Greece Travel Guide

Contents

Introduction

Chapter 1: Greece Travel essentials

Chapter 2: Ten MUST Visit Places In Greece

Chapter 3: Famous Greek Architectural Wonders

Chapter 4: Best Beaches in Greece

Chapter 5: Itineraries

Chapter 6: Best Restaurants and Cuisine in Greece

Chapter 7: Where To Stay In Greece

Chapter 8: Common Night Destinations & Festivals in Greece

Chapter 9: Souvenirs And Shopping In Greece

Conclusion

Introduction

Greece is a tiny country in Southeast Europe that was once home to one of the greatest civilizations in history. Greece was producing plays and writing dramas at a time when the majority of Europe was experiencing a cultural void. Those renowned Greek sculptors and architects were producing temples and statues of unrivaled beauty. Greece is ranked in the top 20 countries in the world as one of the most popular tourist destinations. Geographically speaking, it is a beautiful location to travel to, with a mountainous mainland and picture-perfect island beaches. Its ancient civilization had a big impact on politics, the Olympics, the arts, language, philosophy, and other fields. Greece is a country of wonders because of its stunning natural landscape, which includes mountains, islands, and beaches. Its pleasant weather plays a significant role in the honor of this nation because of the many natural beauties and the distinctive contrast between sea and land. Many first-time travelers arrive in Greece with preconceived notions and are dismayed to see such a diverse religious and architectural landscape. Only one area of the nation is known for its famed whitewashed houses and lovely blue-domed churches.

Greece is renowned for its amazing natural beauty and fascinating history. It is one of Europe's top travel destinations due to the abundance of islands, beautiful beaches, historic archaeological monuments, and a warm Mediterranean environment. Greeks are all about their love for olives, making them the third-largest producers of olive oil in the world, which is known for its purity, superb flavor, and high nutritional content. In this nation, Mediterranean cuisine is at its finest, and each region of Greece has its unique specialties. Together, the sea, the sand, and the inventiveness of the locals create flavors that will help you create some of the most treasured memories. About From the top attraction Delphi among the 18 UNESCO World Heritage Sites to the breathtaking sunset and dramatic views in Santorini and the extreme and well-known nightlife in Mykonos, Greece holds a place with its own distinctiveness and endearing ambience that draws tourists from all over the world to this exotic country. There are many opportunities to celebrate for travelers who are visiting the country with great joy and anticipation, as there are many enjoyable tourist destinations that offer a variety of pleasures depending on the visitors' preferences. And on sometimes, the reality they encounter supersedes this expectation. Greece can be imagined in many different ways, and there are plenty of stories about it floating about, but the only way to truly comprehend it is to actually visit there and experience its atmosphere for yourself.

Chapter 1:
Greece Travel essentials

Before traveling to Greece, here are some important things you should know:

- Visa Requirements: You could require a visa to enter Greece, depending on your nationality. Make sure to research the visa requirements in advance and submit your application as necessary.
- The Euro (€) is the official unit of exchange in Greece. Even while most locations accept credit cards, it's still a good idea to carry some cash with you, especially for smaller businesses.
- Greek is used as the official language. Even while many Greeks, especially in tourist regions, are fluent in English, it never hurts to learn a few simple Greek words and phrases or carry a translation software to make communication easier.
- Ideal Season to Visit: Greece's summer months, from June through August, are the busiest for tourists because of the scorching weather and crowded beaches. Visit during the spring (April to June) or the fall (September to October) for more comfortable temps and less traffic.
- Greece experiences scorching summers and mild winters due to its Mediterranean environment. However, there are regional variations in weather patterns. When visiting the islands in the summer, be ready for soaring temperatures and severe winds, particularly in the Cyclades.
- Bring clothes that will work for the climate there. Greece has a Mediterranean environment, therefore it is best to wear light, breathable clothing, especially in the summer. Don't forget to pack a hat, sunscreen, swimsuit, and comfy walking shoes.

- Greece has a sophisticated system for getting around. The main cities and islands are connected by domestic planes, ferries, buses, and railroads. It's crucial to double verify schedules in advance, especially for ferries since weather might alter them.
- Island hopping: The stunning islands of Greece are well-known. To see the varied culture, landscapes, and beaches, think about include island hopping in your schedule. The Cyclades, Dodecanese, Ionian Islands, and Crete are well-known island chains.
- Greece is well-known for its extensive history and ancient ruins. Among the historical landmarks that are a must-see are the Acropolis and Parthenon in Athens, the ancient city of Delphi, and the Palace of Knossos in Crete.
- Greeks are renowned for their warm hospitality and passion for good meals. Respect the regional customs and traditions by shaking hands when you meet someone, paying respect to sacred places, and dining on regional food. Tipping is customary, and a general rule of thumb is 10%.
- Greece is generally a safe place to travel. But it's always a good idea to use common sense safety measures, including keeping an eye on your possessions, avoiding isolated areas at night, and being wary of pickpockets in busy tourist destinations.
- Make sure you have enough travel insurance that includes medical coverage for your health and safety. Carry any necessary drugs, and if you're an EU citizen, think about getting an EHIC (European Health Insurance Card).
- Respect for Monuments and Nature: When seeing historical monuments or unspoiled landscapes, show consideration for the environment and adhere to any rules or regulations that may be in place. For the enjoyment of future generations, aid in maintaining the beauty.
- Language and Interaction: Greek is the official tongue of Greece. Despite the fact that English is widely spoken in tourist regions, it can be useful to have a pocket phrasebook or utilize a translation app while interacting with locals.
- The earliest writing system still in use today is Greek. Greek, along with Latin, English, and Spanish, is regarded as one of the most influential languages in the world with approximately 5,000 years of continuous usage.
- The Greek equivalent of Christmas is Orthodox Easter: Greece's Christmas is undoubtedly a sight to behold. However, if you can, try to visit us at Easter. Easter, their most significant religious holiday, is primarily spent with family gathered around a table with delicious food and wine or beer. This is actually a national holiday, and people travel back to their hometowns or islands for celebrations. The entire nation closes down to honor the occasion and enjoy family time.
- Greeks are renowned for their friendly hospitality. It is traditional to shake hands upon greeting and keep eye contact throughout conversations. In restaurants, tipping of about 10% is customary.
- Here are some basic Greek words that may be useful if you're a visitor in Greece:

1. Hello/Goodbye:
   - γεια σας (ya sas) - formal
   - γεια σου (ya su) - informal
2. Please: παρακαλώ (para-ka-loh)
3. Thank you: ευχαριστώ (ef-ha-ri-stoh)
4. Yes: ναι (neh)
5. No: όχι (oh-hee)
6. Excuse me: συγνώμη (si-no-mee)
7. Sorry: συγνώμη (si-no-mee)
8. Do you speak English?: Μιλάτε Αγγλικά; (Mee-LAH-teh Ang-lee-KAH?)
9. I don't understand: Δεν καταλαβαίνω (Den ka-ta-la-VENO)
10. Where is...?: Πού είναι...; (Poo EE-ne...?)
- For example: Where is the bathroom? Πού είναι η τουαλέτα; (Poo EE-ne ee too-a-LE-ta?)
11. How much does it cost?: Πόσο κοστίζει; (POH-so kos-TEE-zee?)
12. Can you help me?: Μπορείτε να με βοηθήσετε; (Boh-REH-teh nah meh vee-thee-SEH-teh?)
13. I would like...: Θα ήθελα... (Tha EE-theh-la...)
- For example: I would like a coffee. Θα ήθελα έναν καφέ. (Tha EE-theh-la EH-nan kah-FEH.)
14. Cheers!: Στην υγειά μας! (Steen ee-YAH mas!)
15. Good morning: Καλημέρα (kah-lee-MEH-ra)
- Good afternoon/evening: Καλησπέρα (kah-lee-SPER-a)
- Goodnight: Καληνύχτα (kah-lee-NEE-h-ta)

Chapter 2:
Ten MUST Visit Places In Greece

1. Athens

Greece's capital city, Athens, is a fascinating place to visit since it combines ancient history with contemporary metropolitan activity. Here are some interesting facts about Athens along with its well-known tourist attractions and enticing attractions:

- Athens is one of the world's oldest cities, having a long history dating back more than 3,000 years. It is often considered as the origin of Western culture and the birthplace of democracy.
- Acropolis: Perched atop a rocky outcrop above the city, the Acropolis is a famous ancient citadel. The Parthenon, the Erechtheion, and the Temple of Athena Nike are just a few of the well-known buildings that call this city home. A must-see sight, the Acropolis provides stunning vistas of Athens.
- Parthenon: The Parthenon is a historic temple devoted to the goddess Athena that is located atop the Acropolis. It is a work of art in architecture and a persisting representation of ancient Greece. Visitors can wander the ruins and see the famed structure's unique detailing.
- Athens' Plaka is a lovely district distinguished by its winding, serpentine lanes, neoclassical structures, and lively atmosphere. By way of its classic Greek tavernas, gift shops, and scenic courtyards, it provides an insight into the city's past. It seems like traveling back in time to explore Plaka.

- National Archaeological Museum: The National Archaeological Museum is a must-see location for history buffs. It contains a sizable collection of ancient Greek items, including jewelry, ceramics, sculptures, and relics from many Greek archaeological sites.
- The Ancient Agora, which served as a market, political hub, and gathering spot, was the core of ancient Athens. Today, tourists can explore the remains and go to the Stoa of Attalos, an old structure that currently serves as a museum with Agora relics on show.
- Modern City Life: Athens is a bustling, modern city that is nonetheless steeped in history. Visitors can take in the city's busy nightlife and culinary options, explore trendy neighborhoods like Exarcheia and Koukaki, or enjoy the city's flourishing street art scene.
- Athens Riviera: Conveniently located in the city center, the Athens Riviera is home to stunning beaches, opulent resorts, and waterfront dining. Visitors can take advantage of the water activities available, relax by the beautiful waters, or stroll down the promenade while taking in the breathtaking views of the Aegean Sea.
- Greek Cuisine: With its extensive selection of traditional Greek dishes and foreign cuisine, Athens is a food lover's heaven. Visitors can take a culinary tour of Athens that includes souvlaki, moussaka, fresh seafood, and delectable pastries.
- Greeks are renowned for their friendly and cordial hospitality. Friendly residents willing to share their culture and assist visitors in making the most of their stay are to be expected in Athens.

2. Thessaloniki

The second-largest city in Greece is Thessaloniki. It is a dynamic city with a deep history, a wide range of cultures, and many attractions that make it a well-liked travel destination. Here are some essential details about Thessaloniki and its top attractions that lure tourists from all over the world:

- Thessaloniki has a fascinating history that spans more than 2,300 years, which is of historical significance. It was established in 315 BC and given the name Thessaloniki by Cassander, an Alexander the Great general. Numerous civilizations have had an impact on the city over the course of its history, including the Romans, Byzantines, Ottomans, and more, leaving behind a variety of historical sites.
- UNESCO World Heritage Sites: There are a number of UNESCO World Heritage Sites in Thessaloniki that history buffs must see. Thessaloniki's Paleochristian and Byzantine Monuments contain well-known structures like the Church of Agios Dimitrios, the Galerius Rotunda, and the Galerius Arch.
- White Tower: The White Tower is Thessaloniki's most recognizable landmark. This cylindrical tower, which was constructed during the Ottoman era, stands tall on the seafront and provides sweeping views of the city and the Thermaic Gulf. There is a museum that displays Thessaloniki's history inside the tower.

- Aristotelous Square: Thessaloniki's main square and a popular gathering spot, Aristotelous Square. It is the center of the social and cultural life of the city and is lined with cafes, boutiques, and stunning neoclassical structures. Visitors can take a leisurely stroll, observe locals, or indulge in nearby food and shopping.
- Ano Poli (Upper Town): Perched on a hill with a view of the city, Ano Poli is Thessaloniki's historic center. It is a lovely area with tiny cobblestone lanes, classic homes, and walls from the Byzantine era. Visitors can visit ancient sites like the Trigoniou Tower and the Church of Osios David while exploring Ano Poli to get a sense of the city's past.
- Museums: Thessaloniki is home to a wide range of museums that serve a range of interests. Thessaloniki's Archaeological Museum is home to a sizable collection of ancient Macedonian artifacts, including magnificent gold jewels. The Museum of Byzantine Culture, the Museum of the Macedonian Struggle, and the Museum of Modern Art are a few further noteworthy institutions.
- Dynamic Nightlife: Thessaloniki is well known for having a dynamic nightlife. Trendy pubs, clubs, live music venues, and classic taverns are just a few of the city's entertainment offerings. Particularly well-liked for its bustling ambiance and superb dining options, the lively Ladadika neighborhood.
- Festivals & Events: Throughout the year, Thessaloniki is home to a number of festivals and events. One of the most esteemed film festivals in Southeast Europe is the Thessaloniki International Film Festival, which takes place every November. The Dimitria Festival, which honors the patron saint of the city, features theater productions, concerts, and exhibitions.
- Thessaloniki offers a wonderful culinary scene, making it a delight for food aficionados. The city is renowned for its scrumptious souvlaki, bougatsa (a classic pastry), and the regional beverage known as tsipouro. It is possible to sample local specialties and fresh products by exploring the city's marketplaces, like Modiano and Kapani.
- Distance from Other Attractions: Thessaloniki is a great starting point for visiting other alluring locations in Northern Greece. The archaeological site of Vergina, where the tomb of Philip II (Alexander the Great's father) was found, and Mount Olympus, the fabled abode of the ancient Greek gods, are two nearby attractions.

3. **Santorini**

Greece's gorgeous island of Santorini is part of the Aegean Sea and is renowned for its extraordinary scenery, breathtaking views, and fascinating past. Following are some interesting facts about Santorini, along with travel recommendations and the island's top attractions:

- Geological Wonder: The crescent-shaped shape of Santorini was created by a volcanic explosion that took place about 3,600 years ago. One of Santorini's distinguishing characteristics, the caldera is a sizable volcanic crater that offers breathtaking views.
- Beautiful scenery: The island is well-known for its charming whitewashed structures, blue-domed churches, and winding, little lanes. A magnificent and recognizable scene is produced by the buildings' strikingly different colors and the azure water.
- Stunning Sunsets: Santorini is well known for its captivating sunsets. The settlement of Oia, positioned on the island's northernmost point, is well-known for its stunning views of the setting sun over the Aegean Sea.
- Beautiful Beaches: Santorini is home to distinctive beaches with breathtaking scenery. The most well-liked options include Red Beach, distinguished by its reddish cliffs, and Perissa Beach, distinguished by its black volcanic sand. Tourists also adore the beaches of Kamari and Perivolos.
- Visitors can tour historical landmarks and ancient ruins on the island, which is rich in history. The "Minoan Pompeii" is a term that is frequently used to refer to Akrotiri, a Bronze Age settlement that has been preserved by volcanic ash. On a mountaintop, Ancient Thera's remains provide sweeping views.
- Local Food and Wine: Santorini is well known for its mouthwatering cuisine and distinctive regional products. The peculiar flavors of the island's fruits, vegetables, and wines are a result of the soil's volcanic composition. Don't pass up the chance to sample Assyrtiko, a well-known local white wine.

- Destination for Romance: Santorini is frequently considered as one of the world's most romantic locations. It is a popular destination for honeymooners and couples because of its gorgeous scenery, opulent accommodations, and cozy atmosphere.
- Adventure and Activities: Visitors can partake in a number of activities in addition to admiring the island's natural beauty. Take a sailing cruise around the caldera or go scuba diving to see the underwater ecosystem. Hikers can take use of beautiful pathways like the Fira to Oia path.
- Santorini is filled with lovely towns that are worth exploring. Villages like Imerovigli, Pyrgos, and Megalochori, in addition to Oia and Fira (the capital), provide an insight into the island's traditional way of life and boast breathtaking vistas.
- Greek hospitality is renowned worldwide, and Santorini is no exception. The island's rich cultural legacy and the friendly and hospitable residents all add up to an amazing experience.

4. Meteora Monasteries

The Meteora Monasteries are an extraordinary and inspiring location that draws visitors from all over the world to central Greece, close to the town of Kalambaka. Here are some details on the Meteora Monasteries and some of the factors that make them so popular with tourists.:

- The Meteora Monasteries are highly significant from a religious and historical standpoint. They were initially constructed by Orthodox monks who desired seclusion and seclusion in the 14th and 15th centuries. During a period of political unrest, the monasteries acted as refuges for the soul and as educational institutions.
- Meteora Monasteries are a UNESCO World Heritage Site, honored for its historic relevance, architectural brilliance, and magnificent natural beauty.
- Beautiful Location: The Meteora Monasteries are distinguished by their beautiful location. They are placed on enormous granite pillars, which produces an incredible and dramatic scene. With their distinctive shapes and sizes, the rocks' geological formation is a sight to behold.
- Visitors to the Meteora Monasteries can learn about the history and manner of life of the monks. Some monasteries are still in use today, housing monks and nuns who live and practice their religion there. The religious items, manuscripts, and works of art housed in the monasteries' museums provide a window into their rich past.
- Panoramic Views and Photography Opportunities: The monasteries offer truly stunning panoramic views. Visitors can take in expansive views of the Pindus Mountains, cliffs, and neighboring valleys. For those who enjoy taking photographs, Meteora is a photographer's dream.

- Hiking and nature exploration: Meteora has amazing outdoor recreation and nature exploration opportunities. Visitors can get a close-up view of the area's splendor on the hiking paths. Visitors can see uncommon species of birds as they stroll along the picturesque walkways and take in the distinctive flora and fauna.
- Cultural and Architectural Wonder: The monastery' architecture is remarkable in and of itself. The buildings, which were built on top of the rocks, mix in well with the surroundings. The excellent Byzantine art and workmanship of the time are displayed in the frescoes and interior decorations.
- Film and Pop Culture Connections: A number of films, including the James Bond film "For Your Eyes Only," have included scenes from the Meteora Monasteries. The monasteries' fame has also been increased by the fact that they serve as the iconic background for various music videos, documentaries, and travel-related television programs.
- Guided Excursions & Experiences: Guests can join guided tours to see the monasteries and discover their spiritual significance as well as their history. In-depth explanations of the monastic way of life and local tales are given by knowledgeable guides.
- Peace and Serenity: The Meteora Monasteries provide a tranquil and calm setting. The remote area is surrounded by nature and offers a respite from the busyness of modern life. The serene atmosphere of the monasteries serves as a source of comfort and spiritual inspiration for many tourists.

Visiting the Meteora Monasteries is a unique experience that combines history, spirituality, natural beauty, and cultural exploration. It's no wonder that they attract countless tourists who are captivated by their mystical charm and breathtaking setting.

5. Mykonos

A well-liked tourist resort in Greece's Cyclades islands is Mykonos. Mykonos draws tourists from all over the world because of its exciting nightlife, gorgeous beaches, and endearing traditional architecture. The following are some important details about Mykonos and its top attractions:

- Gorgeous Beaches: Mykonos is renowned for its gorgeous beaches with blue waves and golden sand. Paradise Beach, Super Paradise Beach, Psarou Beach, and Platis Gialos are a few of the most well-known beaches. These beaches include a wide range of water sports, beach clubs, and breathtaking sunset views.
- Charming Mykonos Town, commonly referred to as Chora or Mykonos Town, is the island's capital and is a charming maze of winding alleyways, whitewashed structures, and brightly colored doors and window frames. Its attractiveness is enhanced by the town's famous windmills. The town's abundance of specialty stores, galleries, cafes, and restaurants contributes to its dynamic and colorful atmosphere.
- Little Venice: Little Venice is a district in Mykonos Town that provides breathtaking ocean views. Buildings in this area are constructed close next to the ocean, and some even have balconies that overlook the water. It's a well-liked location to enjoy a meal or beverage while taking in the stunning sunset.

- Delos Island: Delos is a small island with significant historical and archaeological interest that is only a short boat journey from Mykonos. It is a UNESCO World Heritage Site and regarded as one of Greece's most significant archaeological sites. Visitors can explore ancient ruins in Delos, including temples, homes, and statues, which is thought to be the location of the birthplaces of Apollo and Artemis.
- Dynamic Nightlife: Mykonos is well known for its exciting and vivacious nightlife. The island is home to a large number of nightclubs, bars, and beach clubs that host events and provide entertainment all night long. Famous nightlife locations include Scandinavian Bar, Cavo Paradiso, and Paradise Club.
- Water Sports and Activities: Mykonos caters to adventure seekers with a variety of water sports and activities. Jet skiing, windsurfing, paddleboarding, scuba diving, and snorkeling are among the activities you can enjoy. There are places to rent gear and take lessons on several beaches.
- Cosmopolitan Ambiance: Mykonos boasts a hip and cosmopolitan atmosphere that draws international celebrities, fashionistas, and artists. Throughout the year, it organizes a variety of cultural events, art exhibits, and music festivals, enhancing its appeal as a hip destination.
- Gourmet Dining: Mykonos has a thriving restaurant and taverna scene offering a variety of Greek and international cuisines. Visitors can enjoy a variety of delectable gastronomic experiences, from traditional Greek cuisine to gourmet fusion concoctions.
- Luxury Accommodations: There are many different types of accommodations available on Mykonos, including boutique hotels, luxury resorts, and lovely villas. Many accommodations provide breathtaking Aegean Sea views, private pools, and upscale amenities to guarantee a relaxing and opulent stay.
- Mykonos has a long history of being regarded as an LGBT-friendly vacation spot. It boasts a thriving LGBT scene with gay-friendly pubs, clubs, and events, especially in Mykonos Town.

6. Samaria Gorge

Greece, notably the island of Crete, is home to the amazing natural feature known as the Samaria Gorge. The Samaria Gorge has a number of interesting facts, as well as well-known highlights and reasons why it's worthwhile to visit.

- The Samaria Gorge is one of the longest canyons in Europe, measuring over 16 kilometers (10 miles) in length. It is located in Crete's southwest, near the White Mountains (Lefka Ori).
- Samaria National Park, also known as the Samaria Gorge National Park, was established in 1962.
- Approximately 48 square kilometers (19 square miles) in size, the park is home to a variety of plants and animals.
- Scenic Beauty: With its high cliffs, rough terrain, and thick vegetation, the gorge offers spectacular natural beauty.

- The "Iron Gates," a tiny corridor with sheer rock walls as high as 300 meters (984 feet), is one of the breathtaking vistas that visitors can explore.
- The Samaria Gorge is a well-known trekking location that draws outdoor enthusiasts and nature lovers.
- The trail descends through the valley to the settlement of Agia Roumeli on the Libyan Sea coast from the trailhead at Xyloskalo, which is 1,230 meters (4,035 ft) above sea level.
- A diversity of plant species, including rare Cretan endemics like the Cretan ebony (ebenus cretica) and the wild Cretan tulip, can be found in the gorge (tulipa saxatilis).
- The Cretan wild goat (kri-kri), different bird species, and reptiles are among the local wildlife.
- The Samaria Gorge has historical and cultural value because there are still ruins of ancient towns and churches there.
- Within the national park, the deserted settlement of Samaria, after which the gorge is called, provides a window into the past.
- The Samaria National Park is committed to preserving and safeguarding its distinctive environment.
- While enjoying the pure natural settings, visitors can learn about and support conservation activities.
- Tourist Attractions: Traveling down the Samaria Gorge offers an exciting and satisfying trip that enables guests to fully appreciate nature's beauty. The breathtaking scenery, the strenuous but energizing hike, the chance to see rare plants and animals, and the opportunity to see historical places are just a few of the highlights.
- Accessibility & Season: From May through October, when the park is open to the public, visitors can enter the Samaria Gorge.
- To avoid intense heat and crowded areas, spring or autumn are the best times to visit.
- Practical Points: Hiking the Samaria Gorge calls for good physical condition as well as the appropriate hiking supplies, such as strong boots and sun protection.
- It's crucial to be ready and take the proper precautions because the trail can be difficult and has high, uneven terrain.
- The Samaria Gorge in Greece is a must-see location for nature lovers and people looking for a distinctive way to enjoy the breathtaking scenery of Crete. It offers a memorable experience of natural beauty, cultural history, and outdoor adventure.

7. Corfu Town

The capital and main city of the Greek island of Corfu is Corfu Town, often called Kerkyra. Here are some details about Corfu Town and the explanations for why it is a well-liked vacation spot:

- Historical Importance: Corfu Town has a long, illustrious past that goes back to prehistoric times. Greek, Roman, Byzantine, Venetian, and British civilizations, among others, have had an impact on the city. Its historical landmarks and architectural design showcase this rich past.

- The Old Town of Corfu, which includes Corfu Town, was named a UNESCO World Heritage Site in 2007. The Old Town draws tourists from all over the world with its Venetian-style buildings, winding lanes, and attractive squares.

- The Old Fortress and the New Fortress, two outstanding Venetian fortresses, are located in Corfu Town. The Old Fortress, perched atop a rocky outcropping, provides sweeping views of both the city and the ocean. On a hilltop above the village, The New Fortress offers a view into the island's former defensive history.

- Liston Promenade: The Liston is a stunning promenade in Corfu Town that was modeled after Paris's Rue de Rivoli. With cafes, restaurants, and shops, it has magnificent arched buildings. Locals and visitors alike frequently unwind, enjoy a cup of coffee, and take in the lively environment at The Liston.

- Spianada Square is situated close to the Liston and is the biggest square in the Balkans. Cricket matches, concerts, and other cultural events are held in the square, which is a centre of activity. It's a terrific spot to people-watch and take in Corfu Town's buzzing vibe.

- Corfu Town is home to a number of museums and cultural attractions that are well worth visiting. Artifacts from ancient Corfu are on display in the Archaeological Museum of Corfu, while a sizable collection of works by artists from China, Japan, and India are on view in the Museum of Asian Art. Another must-see site is the Church of Saint Spyridon, which is devoted to Corfu's patron saint.

- Corfu Town has a variety of dining establishments as well as local and foreign retailers. There are numerous stores selling apparel, jewelry, souvenirs, and other items along the city's main shopping streets, such as Kapodistriou and Nikiforou Theotoki. Additionally, Corfu Town is also known for its fantastic dining options, with a wide variety of eateries serving both traditional Greek and other cuisines.
- Corfu Town comes alive after dark and offers a thriving nightlife scene. Everyone may find something to enjoy, from quaint bars and classic taverns to chic clubs and live music places. Streets like Liston and Old Town are especially well-liked for evening strolls and sipping a few drinks.
- Corfu Town doesn't have any sandy beaches, although it is ideally adjacent to some of the island's breathtaking coastline. Beautiful beaches like Glyfada, Paleokastritsa, and Agios Gordios can be easily reached by car or bus for visitors who are willing to travel a little distance.
- Corfu International Airport is located in Corfu Town, making it simple for travelers from around the world to reach the island. It serves as a starting point for exploring the remainder of the island because to its handy location and good transit connections.

Corfu Town, with its blend of history, culture, stunning architecture, and lively atmosphere, offers a delightful experience for visitors, making it a must-visit destination in Greece.

8. Zagorohoria and the Ancient Ruins of Kassope and Nikopolis.

Northwest Greece's Pindus Mountains contain the hilly region of Zagori, commonly referred to as Zagorohoria. It is a breathtaking location renowned for its unspoiled landscapes, historic towns, and outdoor pursuits. The ancient ruins of Kassope and Nikopolis, which provide a look into Greece's rich historical past, are two of the key attractions in the Zagori region. Here are some details and important information about Zagorohoria and these historic ruins:

- 46 traditional villages make up Zagorohoria, a region tucked away in the Zagori mountain range. Beautiful natural scenery, stone-built homes, stone arches, and cobblestone pathways define the area. For those who enjoy the outdoors, hiking, and adventure, it is a well-liked vacation.
- Kassope's Ancient Ruins: The ancient city of Kassope is situated in the Zagorohoria region of Epirus. It offers impressive archaeological remains and was established in the 4th century BC. The theater, agora (marketplace), temples, and defensive walls may all be explored by tourists. The property offers spectacular panoramic vistas.
- Ancient Ruins of Nikopolis: In the Zagorohoria region, close to Preveza, Nikopolis —which means "Victory City"—is a noteworthy archaeological site. At order to remember his triumph over Mark Antony and Cleopatra in the Battle of Actium, the Roman Emperor Augustus constructed it in 31 BC. A theater, stadium, odeon, Roman baths, and the majestic Octagon Monument are among the remnants.

- Historical Importance: Kassope and Nikopolis are both very important historical sites. In ancient Greece, Kassope was a significant city-state that had a significant impact on both trade and politics in the area. On the other hand, Nikopolis was a vibrant Roman metropolis and a significant cultural hub at the period.
- In addition to their historical significance, the sites of these ancient remains are breathtakingly gorgeous. Kassope, which offers amazing views of the surrounding area, is perched on a hill overlooking a valley. Nikopolis is close to the Ambracian Gulf and offers beautiful views of the surrounding landscape and the ocean.
- Outdoor Activities: There are many chances for outdoor activities in Zagorohoria and the surrounding areas of Kassope and Nikopolis. Visitors can engage in outdoor activities like rafting and kayaking on the Voidomatis River, hike, climb, and mountaineer in the Pindus Mountains, and visit the neighboring Vikos Gorge, one of the deepest gorges in the world.
- Local Customs and Hospitality: Zagorohoria is well known for its friendly people and manner of life. By staying in conventional guesthouses, sampling regional cuisine, and taking part in cultural activities and festivals, tourists can get a taste of the local way of life.

Visiting Zagorohoria and exploring the ancient ruins of Kassope and Nikopolis offers a unique combination of natural beauty, historical significance, and outdoor adventure. It provides a memorable experience for tourists interested in Greece's ancient history and picturesque landscapes.

9. Nafplio

Beautiful Nafplio is a town in Greece's Peloponnese region. It has significant historical value and a pleasant ambience that draws tourists from all over the world. Here are some details about Nafplio and its top attractions to help you decide if you should go there:

- Historical Significance: Following Greece's independence from the Ottoman Empire in 1828, Nafplio served as the nation's first capital. The town has a long history, and the architecture and culture reflect a rich fusion of Venetian, Byzantine, and Ottoman influences.
- The Palamidi Fortress, which is built on a hill above the town of Nafplio, is one of the city's most recognizable features. It provides amazing views of the surroundings and was constructed by the Venetians in the 18th century. The fortress's 999 steps can be climbed by visitors who then have access to its well-preserved bastions, tunnels, and cells.
- The Bourtzi Fortification, which is situated on a little islet in the midst of Nafplio's bay, is another fortress that is well visiting. It was constructed by the Venetians in the fifteenth century as a fortress to guard the town. Bourtzi is now a well-liked tourist destination that can be reached by boat.
- Old Town: The Old Town of Nafplio is a lovely tangle of winding streets, neoclassical structures, and quaint squares. Visitors can unwind and take in the ambiance in one of the cafes or restaurants lining Syntagma Square, the city's largest square. The town's cobblestone lanes are lined with hidden treasures including quaint stores, art galleries, and age-old taverns.

- The oldest section of Nafplio is called Acronauplia, and it has old towers, gates, and walls. Exploring this location provides a window into the town's early

    history. Visitors can take in expansive views of the city, the sea, and the neighboring mountains from Acronauplia.
- Museums: Nafplio is the location of a number of fascinating museums. A variety of local antiquities dating back thousands of years are kept in the Archaeological Museum of Nafplio. In contrast to the Peloponnesian Folklore Foundation Museum, which displays traditional Greek clothing and textiles, the War Museum explores Greece's military history.
- Beaches: The area around Nafplio is endowed with some stunning beaches. With its pristine seas and golden sand, Karathona Beach, just a few kilometers from the town, is a well-liked option. Another beautiful beach, Tolo Beach, is nearby and is well-known for its lengthy sandy beachfront.
- Events and Festivals: Throughout the year, Nafplio is home to a number of festivals and cultural gatherings. The Nafplio Festival takes place in the summer and features performances of music, theater, and dance at distinctive locations all across the city. The Armata Festival, which takes place in September, honors a famous naval conflict and features a festive celebration with fireworks and a live performance.

10. Medieval Town of Rhodes

One of the best-preserved medieval towns in Europe is the Medieval Town of Rhodes, which is situated on the Greek island of Rhodes. It is a UNESCO World Heritage Site. The following information about the town, its tourist attractions, and reasons to go there:

- Historical Importance: The Knights Hospitaller founded the medieval town of Rhodes in the 14th century, and it served as their headquarters of operations while fighting in the Crusades. It was a key location in the history of the Eastern Mediterranean and was home to many different civilizations and cultures over the years.
- Impressive Fortifications: The Knights Hospitaller built the massive medieval walls that surround the town, which are regarded as among of the best examples of fortifications from that time period. There are seven gates along the roughly 4-kilometer-long walls, and each gate has a distinct personality.
- Palace of the Grand Master: The Palace of the Grand Master is one of the town's most notable landmarks. It was initially constructed in the 14th century and used to house the Grand Master of the Knights Hospitaller. It now serves as a museum with a view of the town and a collection of medieval antiques.
- Street of the Knights: The inns of the many knightly orders, including the Knights of Saint John, who originally resided in Rhodes, line this charming cobblestone street. The Street of the Knights' setting and architecture transport visitors back to the Middle Ages.
- The Rhodes Archaeological Museum is housed within the city's medieval walls and features a sizable collection of ancient Rhodes artifacts, including pottery, jewelry, and sculptures. It is a fantastic location to learn about the history of the island and the various civilizations that have called it home.
- Gothic Architecture: Magnificent specimens of Gothic architecture may be seen in the Medieval Town of Rhodes. These structures are distinguished by their exquisite stonework, vaulted ceilings, and ornate façade. Visitors can see the intricate craftsmanship of the medieval era while strolling through the winding streets.
- Beautiful Byzantine churches may be found all across the town, highlighting the Byzantine Empire's impact on the island. Examples of churches with beautiful frescoes and religious icons include the Church of Panagia tou Kastrou and the Church of Agios Fanourios.
- Attractive Atmosphere: The town's winding lanes, which are surrounded with vibrant structures, cute stores, and charming cafes, produce a special and romantic atmosphere. Indulge in regional food, take leisurely strolls, and take in the lively ambiance of this thriving medieval town.
- Acropolis of Rhodes: The Acropolis of Rhodes, which belongs to the Hellenistic era, is located just outside the medieval fortifications. You can visit historic ruins, including a stadium and a temple, and it provides panoramic views of the town and its surroundings.
- Mediterranean Climate: The Medieval Town is located on Rhodes Island, which has a Mediterranean climate with moderate winters and scorching summers. This makes it a great place to visit if you want good weather, gorgeous beaches, and a mix of historical and natural attractions.

The Medieval Town of Rhodes is a captivating destination that seamlessly blends history, culture, and beauty. With its well-preserved medieval architecture, intriguing museums, and a vibrant atmosphere, it offers a unique travel experience for history enthusiasts and those seeking a journey back in time.

Chapter 3:
Famous Greek Architectural Wonders

The Parthenon Temple

One of Greece's most recognizable structures and a UNESCO World Heritage site is the Parthenon Temple. It is an architectural marvel and a representation of ancient Greek culture that may be found on the Acropolis hill in Athens. The Parthenon is described in depth here, along with tourist attractions, fees, regulations, and other pertinent information.:

1. Architecture and History:

- The renowned sculptor Phidias oversaw the construction of the Parthenon between 447 and 432 BCE, during the Golden Age of Athens.
- It was built as a temple for the goddess Athena Parthenos, who was revered as Athens' patron saint.
- The architects Ictinus and Callicrates were in charge of the temple's design, and Phidias was in charge of the decorative artwork and sculptures.
- A Doric temple made entirely of marble, the Parthenon is admired for its outstanding symmetry, pleasing proportions, and exquisite workmanship.

2. Tourist Highlights:

- From its vantage point atop the Acropolis, the Parthenon provides stunning views of Athens and its surroundings.
- Ancient Greek craftsmanship is evident in the temple's architectural details, which include the fluted columns, pediments, friezes, and metopes.
- The Parthenon's west pediment represents the struggle between Athena and Poseidon for control of Athens, while the east pediment shows the birth of Athena.
- A massive statue of Athena created by Phidias and kept at the Parthenon was composed of gold and ivory. Sadly, the statue has vanished.

3. Charges and Opening Hours:

- Adults must pay €20 for general entrance to the Acropolis, which grants them access to the Parthenon.
- Senior citizens and students both receive discounted prices. Under-18s are admitted free of charge.
- Please be aware that these fees could vary, so it's best to check the official websites or get in touch with the authorities for the most recent details.
- Depending on the season, the hours of operation change. The Parthenon typically remains open from 8:00 AM until 8:00 PM in the summer and until 5:00 PM in the winter.

4. Rules and Regulations:

- While visiting the Parthenon, various guidelines and standards must be adhered to in order to protect the historical site.

- No objects or architectural components may be touched or taken away by visitors.
- Tripods, selfie sticks, and other tools that could harm the property are not permitted.
- Vandalism of any kind, including sitting on the columns or climbing the old buildings, is absolutely forbidden.
- For their safety and the preservation of the area, visitors are urged to respect the signs, barriers, and designated walkways.

Erechthion

On Athens' Acropolis, near the Parthenon, stands the ancient Greek temple known as the Erechtheion. It is a recognizable and impressively designed structure that draws lots of tourists every year. Here are some specifics on the Erechtheion.

1. Architecture and Highlights:

- During the Golden Age of Athens, which lasted from 421 to 406 BCE, the Erechtheion was constructed. It was created by Mnesicles, a renowned architect.
- Both Athena Polias and Poseidon-Erechtheus, two significant deities in ancient Greek mythology, are honored in this temple.
- The Erechtheion's porch, sometimes referred to as the Caryatid Porch or Porch of the Maidens, is its most recognizable feature. It is supported by six marble columns that are sculpted with feminine figurines called caryatids.
- The frieze that extends along the temple's exterior walls and features scenes from Greek mythology and history is another noteworthy aspect.
- The architecture of the temple combines several architectural forms, notably the Ionic order and the Erechtheion's own peculiar design, to create a singular structure.
- Visitors are welcome to explore the east chamber, west chamber, and north porch, among other chambers and sanctuaries, inside the Erechtheion.

2. Charges and Opening Hours:

- The Erechtheion and other Acropolis monuments are accessible with the general admission Acropolis ticket. Adult tickets cost about €20, while reduced-price tickets cost about €10. (e.g., students, seniors).
- It's important to keep in mind, though, that rules and ticket prices are subject to change, so it's best to check the official website or get in touch with the local authorities for the most recent details.

3. Rules and Regulations:

- Certain laws and restrictions are normally upheld in order to guarantee the site's preservation and improve visitor safety. These might include limits on touching the historic buildings, smoking bans, and rules against using tripods or flash photography.
- Visitors are urged to stay on authorized trails and to avoid straying into off-limits territory.
- Furthermore, it's critical to respect the site's historical and cultural significance by refraining from littering and inflicting any harm to the buildings.

4. Visitor Tips:

- To avoid crowds and the warmest part of the day during the summer, it is advised to visit the Erechtheion and the Acropolis early in the day or later in the afternoon.
- Since there are stairs and uneven ground, it is best to wear comfortable shoes.
- It is imperative to bring sunscreen, a hat, and drink because the site may be exposed to the sun, especially during the summer.

Temple of Apollo

An old Doric temple in Greece called the Temple of Apollo is devoted to the Apollon divinity. I don't have access to current information or specifics regarding recent updates, but I can give you a general overview of the temple based on what I know about it historically as of September 2021. Before making travel arrangements, it's always a good idea to confirm the most recent information from dependable sources or tourism websites.

Location: The Temple of Apollo, also called the Temple of Delphi, is found in Delphi, a small settlement in central Greece that is perched on the slopes of Mount Parnassus. In the past, Delphi was revered as the center of the globe and was known for its oracle, where people sought the predictions of Apollo.

Tourist Highlights:

- Known for its magnificent Doric architectural style, the Temple of Apollo is a beautifully preserved ancient Greek temple. It has strong limestone columns, a colonnaded facade, and a frieze that depicts numerous mythical episodes. It was built around the 4th century BCE.
- Delphi's extensive archaeological complex also includes the Sanctuary of Athena Pronaia, the Tholos of Delphi, the ancient theater, and the Stadium. This is in addition to the Temple of Apollo. Visitors can get a taste of the theological and cultural significance of ancient Delphi by exploring these ruins.
- The famed Charioteer of Delphi, a bronze figure of a charioteer, is housed in the Delphi Museum, which is close to the archaeological site. Other notable items in the museum's collection include votive offerings and statues that were unearthed during excavations.

Charges and Rules: Please be aware that charges and rules are subject to change at any time, therefore it is important to check with official sources for the most current and correct information. Here are some general principles:

- Entry fees: The archaeological site and the museum typically charge admission. Adults, students, and older citizens may pay different costs. There may occasionally be multi-attraction combination tickets available for the Delphi complex.
- Opening Times: The site and museum normally have set hours of operation, which may change according to the time of year. It's a good idea to check the opening times in advance so you can schedule your visit appropriately.
- Photography and videography: There may be laws governing photography and filming. While shooting photos for personal use is frequently permitted, there can be limitations if the photos are being taken for work or for a business. Tripods or other apparatus might need a special permit.
- Respectful Behaviour: It's crucial to respect the historical significance of the site when visiting the Temple of Apollo and the neighborhood. Avoid destroying or removing any artifacts by paying attention to any instructions or signage that may be there.

Great Theatre of Epidaurus

A prominent ancient theater called the Great Theatre of Epidaurus can be found in the Greek archaeological site of the same name. It is regarded as one of the most remarkable and well-preserved antique theaters in the entire world. The Great Theatre of Epidaurus is described in depth here, along with its tourist attractions, fees, policies, and other pertinent information:

1. Background information: The architect Polykleitos the Younger is credited with designing the Great Theatre of Epidaurus, which was constructed in the fourth century BCE. It was a portion of the Asklepios Sanctuary, a hospital honoring the Greek deity of medicine.

2. Architecture and acoustics: The theater is round and has a seating capacity of about 14,000 people. Because of its outstanding acoustics, even a stage whisper may be heard across the entire theater. The theater's layout enables optimum sound amplification without the use of any electrical equipment.

3. Performances: During the Epidaurus Festival, which takes place every year from July through August, the theater is largely used to hold ancient Greek drama performances. The festival draws theater lovers from all around the world and presents a range of classic plays. It's crucial to remember that the theater occasionally hosts other cultural activities in addition to these shows.

4. Prices and Business Hours: Adult admission to the Great Theatre of Epidaurus costs roughly 12 euros. The location normally opens early in the morning and closes in the late afternoon, though the hours can change depending on the season. For the most recent details on costs and hours of operation, it is advised to consult the official website or get in touch with the local authorities.

5. Rules & Regulations: The following guidelines should be followed when visiting the Great Theatre of Epidaurus:

- It is not permitted to touch or climb the historic buildings.
- The steps leading up to the theater can be steep and uneven, therefore visitors are urged to wear appropriate footwear.
- The use of tripods or professional filming equipment may need a specific permit, however taking pictures for personal use is typically permitted.
- Inside the theater, visitors are required to keep a courteous and calm demeanor.

6. Other Attractions in the Area: In addition to the Sanctuary of Asklepios, the ancient site of Epidaurus also has the Tholos of Epidaurus, a circular structure, and the Epidaurus Museum. These landmarks offer additional insights into the region's ancient history and culture.

Knossos Palace

One of the most significant and well-known historical sites in the nation is the ancient archaeological site of Knossos Palace, which is situated on the Greek island of Crete. The following provides comprehensive information about Knossos Palace, including its tourist attractions, fees, policies, and other pertinent information:

1. Overview: Knossos Palace is an ancient Minoan palace complex that dates back to the Bronze Age. It was the ceremonial and political center of the Minoan civilization, which flourished around 2000 to 1450 BCE. The palace was first constructed around 1900 BCE and was continuously expanded and rebuilt over the centuries.

2. Tourist Highlights:

- Grand Staircase: The Grand Staircase, which leads to the central courtyard, is one of the palace's most spectacular features. It is decorated with vibrant frescoes that show a variety of Minoan life events.

- Throne Room: The Throne Room is thought to have served as the palace's ceremonial and power center. It has colorful frescoes and a rebuilt throne.

- The Queen's Megaron contains well-preserved frescoes of the "Ladies in Blue" and the "Dolphin Fresco," which are assumed to have been the queen's private chambers.

- Royal Road: The Little Palace, which is thought to be a residential neighborhood, is connected to the palace by the Royal Road. Visitors can get a sense of the palace's layout and magnificence by strolling down this path.

- Storage Magazines: The palace contained large "magazines" for storing goods, including wheat, olive oil, and other supplies. You can explore a few of these storage spaces.

3. Charges and Opening Hours:

- Knossos Palace charges an entrance price of 16 euros for adults and 8 euros for discounted admission (students, senior citizens, etc.).

- Please be aware that prices and hours may change, so it's best to check the official website or contact the location for the most recent information.

4. Rules and Regulations:

- Non-commercial photography is typically permitted on the property. Tripods and flash photography, however, could be forbidden or limited in some places.

- Visitors are expected to treat the historical site and its objects with respect. In order to protect the delicate artifacts, it is normally forbidden to touch the frescoes or walls.

- Guided Tours: At Knossos Palace, guided tours are offered. Joining one can help you better appreciate the site's significance and history.

- Facilities for visitors: The location has amenities like restrooms, a small cafe, and a gift shop.

Temple of Hephaestus

The Hephaisteion or Theseion, commonly known as the Temple of Hephaestus, is an ancient Greek temple that may be seen in Athens, Greece, on the western slope of the Acropolis. It is a noteworthy archaeological site and one of the best-preserved Doric temples in the nation. The Temple of Hephaestus is described in depth below, along with tourist attractions, fees, regulations, and other crucial information:

1. History and Architecture:

- In the fifth century BCE, between 449 and 415 BCE, during Pericles' Golden Age, the Temple of Hephaestus was constructed.
- It was dedicated to Hephaestus, the Greek god of fire, metalworking, and workmanship.
- Ictinus, the architect who is also credited with creating the Parthenon, was the designer of the temple.
- The temple's Doric architecture is recognizable by its solid, manly aspect and its straightforward, rectangular floor plan.
- It has a pronaos (porch), a cella (inner chamber), and an opisthodomos and is composed of Pentelic marble (rear chamber).

2. Tourist Highlights:

- Visitors can view a magnificent specimen of classical Greek architecture at the well-preserved historical site known as the Temple of Hephaestus.
- Panoramic views of Athens are available from the temple, including those of the neighboring Acropolis and the surrounding area.
- The remains of the old altar, which was used to offer sacrifices to Hephaestus, may be seen inside the temple.
- Greek mythological events, such as Hercules' labors and the conflict between Theseus and the Centaurs, are depicted on the friezes of the temple.

3. Charges and Opening Hours:

- The combined ticket for the Athens archaeological sites, which costs €20 for adults and is good for five days, includes access to the Temple of Hephaestus. It's always a good idea to double-check for updates or adjustments to entrance prices, though.
- Opening times fluctuate throughout the year, but are normally from dawn till dusk. Prior to your visit, it is essential to establish the precise opening times as they may change owing to seasonal changes or unanticipated events.

4. Rules and Etiquette:

- In order to protect the Temple of Hephaestus for future generations, visitors must abide by the laws and regulations established by the archaeological authorities.
- No parts of the temple's architecture or artifacts may be handled or taken out.
- Observe the warnings and obstacles put in place to safeguard the temple's building.
- In general, photography is permitted, however using tripods or additional lighting can need special authorization.
- As the area around the temple might be uneven, it is advised to dress modestly and wear comfortable shoes.

Temple of Artemis

The magnificent ancient Greek temple known as the Temple of Artemis, sometimes called the Artemision, was devoted to the goddess Artemis. It was situated at Ephesus, a city that is currently a part of Turkey but was once a part of Greece. The temple, which was known for its majesty and beauty, was one of the Seven Wonders of the Ancient World. Even if the temple is no longer standing, I can give you comprehensive information about its historical importance, tourist attractions, fees (if any), laws, and other pertinent specifics.

1. Historical Significance:

- One of the most significant religious structures in the ancient Greek world, the Temple of Artemis was constructed in the sixth century BCE.
- The well-known Greek architect Chersiphron and his son Metagenes were responsible for its creation.
- The Greek goddess Artemis, who is associated with the hunt, wildlife, and fertility, among other things, was honored in the temple.
- It was thought to be a location for devotion and pilgrimage, drawing followers from a great distance.

2. Tourist Highlights:

- Even though the temple is now in ruins, exploring the Ephesus archaeological site offers the chance to discover the remains of this historic marvel.
- The location has the foundation, columns, and sculptures of the temple still standing, providing a glimpse into its previous opulence.
- The adjacent Ephesus Museum and the British Museum in London both house some of the remaining sculptures and relics from the temple.
- Guided tours of Ephesus frequently include a stop at the Temple of Artemis, allowing tourists to see the Great Theater and other magnificent ancient buildings nearby.

3. Charges:

- There are no special fees for visiting the site of the Temple of Artemis because the temple itself is no longer there.
- The area where the temple originally stood is part of Ephesus' wider archaeological site, which may require payment of an entrance fee. Depending on the particular rules and procedures in effect at the time of your visit, the fees may change.
- For the most recent information on entrance fees and other costs, it is advised to contact local tourism bureaus or visit the Ephesus archaeological site's official website.

4. Rules and Guidelines:

- To protect the historical integrity of Ephesus' archaeological site, visitors must adhere to the regulations put forth by the site's administrators.
- Usually, visitors are asked to show respect for the location by not damaging the remains in any way, including by littering or defacing them.
- It is highly forbidden to climb the historic buildings or remove objects from the location.
- For safety concerns, visitors are urged to stay on authorized walkways and to stay out of restricted areas.
- Photography and filming may be permitted for personal use depending on the site and local laws, however using tripods and other professional equipment would need a specific permit.

The Temple of Zeus

The Olympieion, commonly referred to as the Columns of the Olympian Zeus or the Temple of Zeus, is a historic temple that can be seen in Athens, Greece. One of the biggest temples in the nation, it is also a significant archaeological site. Here are some specifics on the Temple of Zeus:

Location: The Temple of Zeus is situated southeast of the Acropolis, in the heart of Athens. It is located within the archaeological site of the ancient city.

Historical Significance: Construction of the temple began in the 6th century BCE but was not completed until the reign of the Roman Emperor Hadrian in the 2nd century CE. It was dedicated to Zeus, the king of the Greek gods and the ruler of Mount Olympus. The temple was a magnificent structure, showcasing the power and grandeur of the gods.

Tourist Highlights: The Temple of Zeus offers visitors a glimpse into ancient Greek architecture and mythology. Although only a few columns remain standing today, they are still awe-inspiring. The temple originally had 104 columns, each reaching a height of approximately 17 meters (56 feet). The sheer scale of the temple is a testament to the ancient Greeks' engineering skills.

Close to the temple, visitors can see the Arch of Hadrian, an imposing marble gateway erected by Emperor Hadrian. It served as a symbolic entrance to the city of Athens.

Charges and Rules: To visit the Temple of Zeus, you need to purchase a ticket for the archaeological site, which includes access to several other ancient landmarks in Athens. the ticket price for the combined archaeological site, including the Acropolis, is around 20 euros for adults. However, please note that ticket prices and rules may change, so it's best to check with the official authorities or tourist information centers for up-to-date information.

When visiting the temple or any other archaeological site, it's important to follow certain rules and guidelines to preserve these historical treasures. Some general rules include:

1. Respect the site: Treat the temple and its surroundings with respect. Do not climb on the ancient structures or touch the ancient stones.
2. No littering: Keep the area clean and dispose of any trash in designated bins.
3. Photography: Feel free to take photographs for personal use, but be mindful not to use flash photography if it's prohibited, as it can cause damage to ancient artifacts.
4. Stay on designated paths: Follow the designated paths and avoid stepping on restricted areas.

It's advisable to check with the official authorities or signage at the site for any specific rules or restrictions that may be in place during your visit.

The Temple of Zeus is a remarkable archaeological site that offers visitors a chance to witness the grandeur of ancient Greek architecture and mythology. Exploring this site can be a captivating experience for history enthusiasts and tourists alike

The Temple of Hera

The Heraion, sometimes referred to as the Temple of Hera, is a historic Greek temple that may be found in Olympia, Greece. The goddess Hera, the mother of the Greek gods and the wife of Zeus, is honored by its dedication. The temple, one of Greece's most important archaeological sites, draws lots of visitors each year. Here are some specifics on the Temple of Hera:

Location: The Temple of Hera is situated within the archaeological site of Olympia, in the western part of the Peloponnese region in Greece. Olympia was the birthplace of the Olympic Games and holds great historical and cultural importance.

Historical Significance: The temple was constructed around the 7th century BCE and underwent several expansions and renovations over the centuries. It was part of the larger sanctuary of Olympia, which included various religious and athletic structures. The Temple of Hera served as a religious center and was used for the worship of Hera during the Olympic Games.

Architectural Features: The Temple of Hera is built in the Doric architectural style, characterized by its simple and sturdy design. It is peripteral, meaning it is surrounded by a single row of columns on all sides. The temple originally had six columns on the front and back, and sixteen columns on the sides. Today, only the remains of these columns and parts of the entablature are visible.

Tourist Highlights: Visiting the Temple of Hera provides an opportunity to explore the ancient ruins and immerse oneself in Greek history. Some highlights include:

- Temple Ruins: Explore the remains of the temple and marvel at the surviving columns and architectural elements that give a glimpse into its past glory.
- Altar of Hera: Located in front of the temple, the altar was used for making offerings and sacrifices during religious ceremonies.
- Archaeological Museum: Within the Olympia site, there is an archaeological museum that houses a collection of artifacts found in the area, including sculptures, statues, and relics from the ancient Olympic Games.

Charges and Rules: To visit the Temple of Hera and the Olympia archaeological site, there is an entrance fee. The exact charges may vary, so it's advisable to check the official website or local tourist information for up-to-date prices. As for rules, visitors are typically expected to adhere to the following guidelines:

- Respect the Site: Treat the ruins with respect and avoid touching or causing damage to the ancient structures.
- No Littering: Keep the site clean by disposing of any trash in designated bins.
- Follow Instructions: Follow any instructions or signs provided by the authorities or guides.
- Photography: Photography is usually allowed, but the use of tripods or professional equipment may require permission or an additional fee.

- Dress Code: While there might not be strict dress codes, it is recommended to dress modestly and comfortably, taking into consideration the cultural and historical significance of the site.

Visiting the Temple of Hera in Greece offers a fascinating insight into ancient Greek civilization, architecture, and mythology. It is a must-visit destination for history enthusiasts and anyone interested in experiencing the rich cultural heritage of Greece.

Odeon of Herodes Atticus

The Herodion, often referred to as the Odeon of Herodes Atticus, is a historic amphitheater that is situated on the southwest side of the Acropolis in Athens, Greece. One of the oldest theaters in the world that has been preserved the best is this one. The Odeon of Herodes Atticus is described in detail below, along with tourist attractions, fees, regulations, and other pertinent information:

1. History and Architecture:

- The Odeon of Herodes Atticus was built in 161 AD by the Athenian magnate Herodes Atticus in memory of his wife.
- The theater was primarily used for musical performances and could accommodate up to 5,000 spectators.
- The structure was originally roofed, but it was destroyed in the 3rd century AD and never rebuilt.
- Today, the Odeon is renowned for its exceptional acoustics and stunning architecture.

2. Tourist Highlights:

- The Odeon of Herodes Atticus is an iconic landmark and a popular tourist attraction in Athens.
- Visitors can marvel at the ancient theater's grand structure, made of Pentelic marble.
- The stage wall and the rows of stone seats are still intact, providing a glimpse into the theater's ancient glory.
- The theater is occasionally used for live performances, including ancient Greek plays, concerts, and cultural events, especially during the Athens & Epidaurus Festival in the summer.

3. Charges and Access:

- Access to the Odeon of Herodes Atticus is included in the combined ticket for the archaeological sites of Athens, which costs €30
- The combined ticket grants entry to several other archaeological sites, including the Acropolis, the Ancient Agora, the Roman Agora, and more.
- The ticket is valid for five days and can be purchased at any of the participating sites.
- It's advisable to check the official website or local tourist information for the most up-to-date information on ticket prices and access.

4. Rules and Regulations:

- To ensure the preservation of the ancient theater, there are certain rules and regulations that visitors must follow.

- Climbing on the seats or any part of the structure is strictly prohibited.
- Visitors are expected to respect the historical significance of the site and refrain from any actions that may damage the theater.
- Photography is allowed, but the use of tripods and professional equipment may require special permission.
- During live performances, specific rules and etiquette may apply, such as no photography or video recording.

5. Nearby Attractions:

- While visiting the Odeon of Herodes Atticus, you can explore other nearby attractions, including the Acropolis, the Parthenon, the Theatre of Dionysus, and the Acropolis Museum.
- These sites offer a deeper insight into ancient Greek history, art, and culture.

Chapter 4:
Best Beaches in Greece

Greece is well-known throughout the world for its stunning beaches. This nation is renowned for its emerald-green waters and white sandy beaches, which provide a stunning contrast and render the nation picture-perfect. Greece has several beaches, mostly distributed over the mainland but also in some of the best Greek islands of the Aegean and Ionian Sea, where you can see some of the best vistas. You will have an amazing trip experience thanks to the inviting, sun-kissed coolness of the crystal-clear water.

Lalaria

The only way to get to the remote and stunning Lalaria Beach is via boat from Skiathos town. Lalaria is an idyllic place with its white sand beaches and breathtaking cliffs rising from the sea. You'll have trouble putting this amazing beach's enchantment into words. It is the emblem of the island, frequently named the most beautiful beach, and is well-known throughout the globe. Numerous people are drawn to the white stones and emerald sea beneath the imposing vertical rocks every day. When the boats arrive, you can spend your time swimming on a pristine, undeveloped beach on the Sporades islands, with only the wild goats grazing on the hill above as your sole company.

Voidokoilia

You may marvel how this picture-perfect beach with its white sand and emerald-green sea managed to form a perfect semicircle. Homer also makes reference to this ideal form of Voidokoilia in The Odyssey. Spend some time exploring the neighborhood and lazing on the golden sand beach. It won't take long, and you'll feel completely at ease. A fortification from the thirteenth century that was constructed on the remains of classical Pylos is located to the south of the shore. Since this region is regarded as a nudist area, the sound end of the beach may appeal to the local naturalists. People who enjoy letting everything hang loose are drawn to this area of the beach.

Canal d'Amour.

One of the most popular beaches in Greece is Canal d'Amour. Young couples that come to enjoy the stunning sunset vista are the main target audience. The lunar rock formations, which are situated between the Sidari and Peroulades, produce three small waterways that resemble canals. The peculiar feature known as Canal d'Amour stands out. They claim that whomever makes it through the little crack in the rock will meet their soul mate waiting for them on the other side. This beach is ideal for snorkeling, swimming, and dicing.

Katsiki Porto

One of the top six beaches in the entire Mediterranean may be found at Lefkas, at the base of a huge, white cliff that glows orange at sunset. Compared to other beaches in Greece, it boasts the most stunning scenery. Relax on one of Greece's most famous beaches as you take in the magnificence of the ocean and its azure blue waters. You can lounge along the relatively short stretch of sand here while renting an umbrella. The best time to visit Porto Katsiki, one of the most popular tourist attractions, is in the early morning, around 8 am. Despite the fact that it could become crowded as the day goes on, you should still schedule some time to visit.

Sarakiniko

A group of volcanic rock covers make up Sarakiniko Beach. This volcanic rock has been shaped into strange shapes by the wind and the waves, giving you the impression that you are walking on the moon. These milky-white, chalk-soft boulders have been shaped into fascinating forms by the sand and waves. As you get farther from the shore, the deep gulf's green water changes to blue water in all its colors. This beach has personality, which makes it among the best in Greece. It is claimed to have gotten its name from the Saracan pirates who sought refuge here and is situated in the northernmost, windiest region of the Greek island of Milos.

Kolymbithres

This well-known beach is tucked away in the bay of Naoussa and features stunning blue-green water, smooth grayish rocks that have been chiseled into fantastical patterns, and tasty golden coves of various sizes. This Paros beach is a forgotten Greek hero. There are several isolated coves surrounded by stunning granite rock where you may relax with your family. A top-notch beachside restaurant serving the catch of the day just adds to the delight. Numerous secluded coves can be found here that can be explored on foot or by swimming, and a variety of facilities are offered for your comfort.

Elafonisi

The little, unspoiled peninsula of Elafonisi is located west of Chania. This beach is well-known for its vibrant pink sand, calm seas, and dense cedar woodland. It is best to travel there by vehicle or boat for a day trip. It is regarded as the island's cleanest and best-maintained beach. The shimmering, ground-up coral-like material is abundant on Elafonisi. The beach is wonderful and clear, and it is a protected natural reserve. Arrive early to relax and take in the beach's splendor since it becomes more crowded as the day wears on. If you enjoy extreme activities, this is the place to go. Windsurfing is a great sport here. Summertime offers ideal surfing conditions practically every day.

Balos

This beach, which is regarded as one of the best in the Mediterranean, is among the most exotic beaches in all of Greece. Balos is essentially located in western Crete, close to Kissamo. The ocean is a stunning combination of blue and green, and the sand is pink and white. The area is given a fairy-tale feel by the islet of Gramvousa and its Venetian castle. It is claimed to have a mythological Greek origin. This breathtaking location, which is near the Balos Lagoon, is also proud of its own historical significance. Hike through the bird reserve, visit the remnants of a castle from the thirteenth century, or go windsurfing on the bay.

Myrtos

This gorgeous beach is located halfway between Assos and Argostoli. This location will transport you to a new dimension thanks to the white sand and little stones, the turquoise waters, and the base of impossibly high cliffs. If you climb the peninsula to the north, you will see some of the breathtaking vistas from here. With its tall surrounding hills and stunning turquoise waves, this westward facing beach is regarded as one of the best beaches in Greece. It also offers some of the most breathtaking sunset views, making Myrtos' natural beauty unequaled in the entire world. Hike to the perch on the northern headland for views over Hollywood. There is plenty of room for everyone on the long and wide Myrtos beach.

Navagio

Navagio, also known as the Shipwreck Beach, is one of Greece's most famous beaches. This beach has a shipwreck legend from the 1980s, yet despite its challenging accessibility, people still flock to it in the summer. The sharp contrast between the beautiful white sand and the deep blue sea mostly draws them in. One of the most picturesque sights you will ever see is at Navagio Beach. With its towering white cliffs, blue ocean, and white sand, the beach where it ran aground creates a stunning scene. You'll be compelled to jump into its breathtakingly clean water.

Chapter 5:
Itineraries

one-week itinerary

Athens, Santorini, and Mykonos might all be visited during a weeklong trip to Greece. Here is a recommended route:

Day 1: Arrival in Athens

- Arrive in Greece's capital city of Athens.
- Discover the Acropolis, the Parthenon, and the Ancient Agora, three of Athens' historical sites.
- While dining at a small taverna, stroll through the lovely Plaka area.

Day 2: Athens

- A sizable collection of Greek artifacts can be seen at the National Archaeological Museum.
- Discover the colorful district of Monastiraki, which is renowned for its flea market and energetic ambiance.
- Visit the Panathenaic Stadium, the site of the first modern Olympic Games, or take a stroll around the lovely National Gardens.

Day 3: Santorini

- Visit Santorini, one of Greece's most stunning islands, by ferry or plane.
- Discover the picturesque Oia village with its recognizable blue-domed churches and breathtaking sunset vistas.
- Visit the historic site of Akrotiri, a Minoan town that has been preserved and covered in volcanic ash.
- A sunset sail around the caldera is fun, or you may unwind on one of the island's well-known black sand beaches.

Day 4: Santorini

- Explore the quaint streets of Fira's capital city, which are lined with stores, cafes, and eateries.
- Take a boat journey to Nea Kameni, a volcanic island, then trek to the crater for sweeping views.
- Visit a traditional winery or one of the island's vineyards to sample the regional wines.

Day 5: Mykonos

- From the lively island of Santorini, take a ferry to Mykonos.
- Discover the picturesque alleyways and white-washed structures that make up Mykonos Town's streets.
- Visit the island's recognizable windmills, which serve as its emblem.
- Unwind on one of Mykonos' stunning beaches, such as Paradise Beach or Super Paradise Beach.

Day 6: Mykonos

- Take a boat journey to the nearby island of Delos, which is home to the mythological birthplaces of Apollo and Artemis and is a UNESCO World Heritage site.
- Enjoy Mykonos' vibrant nightlife, which includes its renowned clubs and seaside bars.
- Try some traditional Greek fare at one of the island's tavernas to get a taste of the regional cuisine.

Day 7: Departure

You might have some free time to explore Mykonos before leaving, depending on the time of your departure.

Return to Athens via ferry or plane to complete your departure.

five days itinerary

If you have five days to spend in Greece, you can focus on exploring Athens and one or two nearby islands. Here's a suggested five-day itinerary:

Day 1: Athens
- As soon as you get there, you can begin exploring Athens.
- Visit the well-known Acropolis and have a look at its historic buildings, such as the Parthenon and the Temple of Athena Nike.
- Explore the old Plaka district, which is renowned for its quaint shops, tavernas, and small lanes.
- Discover the center of ancient Athens, the Ancient Agora, where Socrates and Plato once strolled.

Day 2: Athens
- Visit the National Archaeological Museum, which has a sizable collection of items from the ancient Greek world.
- Discover the Monastiraki area, known for its thriving flea market and energetic ambiance.
- Wander through the lovely Anafiotika neighborhood, a little area with a Cycladic island feel that is situated beneath the Acropolis.

Day 3: Day trip to Hydra or Aegina Option 1: Day trip to Hydra
- Take a ferry from Athens to the lovely island of Hydra, which is devoid of automobiles.
- Discover Hydra, a little village renowned for its waterfront views, tiny streets, and preserved architecture.
- Take a leisurely stroll down the beach and stop by the ancient Hydra Museum.

Option 2: Day trip to Aegina
- Take a ferry from Athens to the lovely island of Aegina, which is noted for its ancient ruins and pistachio plantations.
- A Doric temple from the fifth century BC, the Temple of Aphaia is still in good condition.
- Discover the bustling town of Aegina, indulge in regional cuisine, and unwind on the island's beaches.

Day 4: Island Exploration (Santorini or Mykonos) Option 1: Santorini
- From Athens, take a flight or ferry to Santorini, one of the most well-known and stunning Greek islands.
- Discover the quaint village of Oia, famous for its blue-domed churches, whitewashed structures, and breathtaking sunset vistas.
- Visit the historic site of Akrotiri, a Bronze Age Minoan village that has been preserved beneath volcanic ash.
- Enjoy the regional food while unwinding on the island's distinctive black or red sand beaches.

Option 2: Mykonos
- Take a flight or ferry from Athens to Mykonos, a popular island known for its vibrant nightlife and picturesque beaches.
- Explore the charming streets of Mykonos Town, known for its white-washed buildings and iconic windmills.
- Spend the day relaxing on the island's beautiful beaches, such as Paradise Beach or Super Paradise Beach.
- Experience the lively nightlife of Mykonos, with its famous clubs and beachfront bars.

Day 5: Departure
- Depending on your departure time, you may have some free time to explore the island or return to Athens.
- Take a flight or ferry back to Athens for your departure.

Remember to check ferry and flight schedules in advance and plan accordingly. This itinerary offers a mix of history, culture, and island exploration, allowing you to experience the best of Athens and one or two stunning Greek islands within five days.

Weekend itinerary

If you have a weekend to spend in Greece, it's best to focus on exploring Athens and its nearby attractions. Here's a suggested weekend itinerary:

Day 1: Athens
- As soon as you get there, you can begin exploring Athens.
- Visit the well-known Acropolis and have a look at its historic buildings, such as the Parthenon and the Temple of Athena Nike.
- Explore the old Plaka district, which is renowned for its quaint shops, tavernas, and small lanes.
- Explore the Ancient Agora, the heart of ancient Athens, where Socrates and Plato once walked.
- Enjoy a delicious Greek dinner at a local restaurant.

Day 2: Day trip to Cape Sounion
- Visit Cape Sounion for the day; it's around an hour's drive from Athens.
- Visit the Temple of Poseidon, which is positioned on a cliff above the Aegean Sea and offers stunning sunset views.
- Swim in the pristine seas and explore the local beaches.
- Once back in Athens, spend the evening taking advantage of the exciting nightlife the city has to offer, including the rooftop bars and live music venues.

Day 3: Athens
- Visit the National Archaeological Museum first thing in the morning, where there is a sizable collection of Greek artifacts.
- Discover the Monastiraki area, known for its thriving flea market and energetic ambiance.
- Wander through the lovely Anafiotika neighborhood, a little area with a Cycladic island feel that is situated beneath the Acropolis.
- If you want to learn more about Greek history and culture, go visit the Benaki Museum or the Museum of Cycladic Art.
- Take in the regional cuisine as you say goodbye over dinner at a traditional Greek tavern.

This weekend itinerary allows you to experience the highlights of Athens, including its ancient landmarks, historical neighborhoods, and vibrant culture. While there are many other destinations to explore in Greece, a weekend in Athens provides a taste of the country's rich history and warm hospitality.

Two weeks itinerary

Day 1-3: Athens
- Visit the Acropolis, the Parthenon, and the Ancient Agora, some of Athens' historical landmarks.
- Visit the National Archaeological Museum and the Acropolis Museum.
- Explore Athens' historic Plaka area by foot.
- Dine on Greek food in neighborhood taverns.

Day 4-5: Santorini
- Take a quick flight or a ferry to Santorini.
- Explore Oia, Fira, and Imerovigli, three stunning settlements.
- Visit the volcanic caldera to witness the mesmerizing sunsets.
- Unwind on the beaches with black sand.
- Go on a boat cruise to the surrounding islands of Nea Kameni and Thirassia, which is optional.

Day 6-7: Mykonos
- Take a quick flight or a ferry to Mykonos.
- Discover Chora's famous windmills (Mykonos Town).
- Unwind on Paradise and Super Paradise's beautiful beaches.
- Enjoy the exciting party scene and nightlife.
- Visit the adjacent UNESCO World Heritage site of Delos.

Day 8-10: Crete
- Take a quick flight or a ferry to Crete.
- Investigate the historical sites of Knossos Palace and the Heraklion Archaeological Museum.
- Visit Chania and Rethymno, two quaint historic towns.
- Visit the stunning beaches of Elafonisi and Balos or take a hike through the Samaria Gorge.
- Try local specialties and Cretan food.

Day 11-13: Rhodes
- travel to Rhodes by plane.
- Discover Rhodes' historic Old Town, a UNESCO World Heritage site.
- Visit the Street of the Knights and the Grand Master's Palace.
- Unwind in Lindos and Faliraki beaches.
- Visit the Valley of the Butterflies and the ancient city of Kamiros.

Day 14: Return to Athens
- Go back to Athens by air or ferry.
- Take the day to visit any missed sights or go souvenir shopping.
- In a typical Greek taverna, take pleasure in a farewell dinner.

Chapter 6:
Best Restaurants and Cuisine in Greece

Greece is recognized for its extensive culinary history and wide range of tastes. The nation has a lot to offer in terms of dining experiences, from traditional tavernas serving authentic Greek food to sophisticated restaurants delivering modern interpretations of Mediterranean foods.

Greek food is well-known throughout the world for its mouthwatering flavors and vivid Mediterranean ingredients. Greece's regional specialties, herbs, olive oil, and fresh, seasonal products are all celebrated in the local cuisine. Here are some of the culinary highlights of Greece:

1. Olive Oil: Greece is one of the largest producers of olive oil, and it is a staple ingredient in Greek cuisine. It is used in almost every dish, from salads to cooked dishes, and is known for its exceptional quality.
2. Mezedes: Mezedes are a selection of small dishes that are often served as appetizers or shared plates. They include various dips like tzatziki (yogurt, cucumber, and garlic), melitzanosalata (eggplant dip), and taramasalata (fish roe dip). Other popular mezedes include dolmades (stuffed grape leaves), spanakopita (spinach and feta pastry), and saganaki (fried cheese).
3. Souvlaki and Gyro: Souvlaki and gyro are popular street food items in Greece. Souvlaki typically consists of grilled skewers of marinated meat, such as pork, chicken, or lamb, served with pita bread, tzatziki, and garnishes. Gyro is made from seasoned meat (usually pork or chicken) cooked on a vertical rotisserie and served in a pita with various toppings.
4. Moussaka: Moussaka is a classic Greek dish made with layers of eggplant, minced meat (usually beef or lamb), and topped with a rich béchamel sauce. It is baked to perfection and is a hearty and flavorful dish.

5. Greek Salad: A traditional Greek salad, or horiatiki, is a refreshing combination of tomatoes, cucumbers, onions, peppers, olives, and feta cheese, dressed with olive oil and sprinkled with oregano. It's a staple in Greek cuisine and often served as a side dish or a light meal.
6. Fresh Seafood: With its extensive coastline, Greece offers an abundance of fresh seafood. Grilled octopus, fried calamari, baked fish, and prawn saganaki (prawns cooked in a tomato and feta sauce) are just a few examples of the delicious seafood dishes you can find.
7. Baklava: Baklava is a popular Greek dessert made of layers of filo pastry filled with a mixture of chopped nuts, sugar, and spices, soaked in sweet syrup. It is sweet, rich, and a perfect ending to a Greek meal.
8. Greek Wines: Greece has a long history of wine production, and Greek wines are gaining recognition globally. From crisp whites like Assyrtiko to robust reds like Xinomavro, there is a wide range of Greek wines to explore and pair with your meal.

While it's challenging to narrow down the list to just a few, here are some of the **best restaurants in Greece** that are highly recommended:
1. Funky Gourmet (Athens): This Michelin-starred restaurant in Athens offers an innovative tasting menu that combines Greek ingredients with modern cooking techniques. With its artistic presentations and bold flavors, Funky Gourmet provides a unique gastronomic experience.
2. Argo (Santorini): Located in the picturesque village of Fira, Argo is known for its breathtaking views of the caldera and sunset. This family-run restaurant specializes in fresh seafood dishes, including grilled fish and traditional Greek mezes.
3. Kritamon (Chania, Crete): Situated in the charming Old Town of Chania, Kritamon showcases Cretan cuisine at its finest. The menu features locally sourced ingredients, highlighting the island's renowned olive oil, herbs, and cheeses.
4. Spondi (Athens): Another Michelin-starred establishment, Spondi is considered one of the best fine-dining restaurants in Athens. Its elegant ambiance and impeccable service complement the exquisite French-inspired Mediterranean dishes on offer.
5. Selene (Santorini): Located in the village of Pyrgos, Selene is a long-established restaurant that celebrates the flavors of Santorini and the Cycladic region. The menu focuses on seasonal ingredients and traditional recipes, ensuring an authentic taste of the island.
6. Ta Karamanlidika Tou Fani (Athens): For a more casual dining experience, Ta Karamanlidika Tou Fani is a must-visit. This deli and restaurant in the heart of Athens offers a selection of cured meats, cheeses, and other Greek delicacies, perfect for a quick lunch or a relaxed evening meal.

7. To Palio Hamam (Thessaloniki): Housed in a converted Ottoman-era bathhouse, To Palio Hamam offers a blend of traditional and modern Greek cuisine. The restaurant is known for its creative dishes, cozy atmosphere, and live music performances.

8. Varoulko (Athens): As a pioneer of seafood cuisine in Greece, Varoulko holds a prominent place in the culinary scene. Located in Mikrolimano Marina, this Michelin-starred restaurant presents beautifully crafted seafood dishes with a contemporary twist.

9. Avli (Rethymno, Crete): Avli is situated in a stunning courtyard in Rethymno's old town and offers a combination of Cretan and Mediterranean cuisine. The restaurant's warm ambiance and flavorsome dishes make it a popular choice among locals and visitors alike.

10. Dexamenes Seaside Hotel (Kourouta Beach, Peloponnese): While not strictly a restaurant, Dexamenes Seaside Hotel deserves a mention for its unique dining experience. This boutique hotel in a renovated wine factory provides guests with the opportunity to enjoy delicious food and local wines while admiring the stunning sunset over the Ionian Sea.

Chapter 7:
Where To Stay In Greece

Greece is a well-liked tourism destination because of its spectacular natural scenery, extensive history, and magnificent islands. In terms of lodging, Greece provides a large selection of opulent hotels with first-rate facilities and services. Here are a few of Greece's top hotels for lodging:

1. Amanzoe, Porto Heli: Located in the Peloponnese region, Amanzoe is a luxurious resort offering private villas with stunning sea views. The hotel features a private beach, a world-class spa, a fitness center, and an infinity pool. Guests can enjoy personalized services, including a private chef, butler, and chauffeur.

2. Canaves Oia, Santorini: Situated in the picturesque village of Oia, Canaves Oia is a boutique hotel famous for its stunning views of the Caldera. The hotel offers elegant suites and villas with private pools or plunge pools. Guests can enjoy amenities such as a gourmet restaurant, a spa, a wine cellar, and a rooftop infinity pool.

3. Eagles Palace, Halkidiki: Located in the region of Halkidiki, Eagles Palace is a luxury beachfront hotel offering elegant rooms, suites, and bungalows with sea or garden views. The hotel boasts a private sandy beach, a spa center, a kids' club, multiple restaurants, and a water sports center.

4. Bill & Coo Suites and Lounge, Mykonos: Situated in Mykonos town, Bill & Coo is a boutique hotel known for its contemporary design and impeccable service. The hotel offers luxurious suites with private pools or hot tubs. Guests can enjoy a gourmet restaurant, a stylish lounge bar, a spa, and a stunning infinity pool overlooking the Aegean Sea.

5. Costa Navarino, Messinia: Located in the Peloponnese, Costa Navarino is a luxury resort complex offering two 5-star hotels: The Romanos and The Westin Resort Costa Navarino. The resort features spacious rooms and suites, multiple restaurants, golf courses, a spa, sports facilities, and access to private beaches.
6. Grace Santorini, Santorini: Perched on a cliffside in Santorini, Grace Santorini is a boutique hotel known for its minimalist design and breathtaking views of the Caldera. The hotel offers stylish suites with private plunge pools or hot tubs. Guests can enjoy a gourmet restaurant, a champagne lounge, and a spa.
7. Domes of Elounda, Crete: Situated in Elounda, Crete, Domes of Elounda is a luxury resort offering spacious suites, villas, and residences with private pools or hot tubs. The resort features a private sandy beach, multiple restaurants, a spa, a kids' club, and a variety of water sports activities. the resort provides a dedicated Kids Club with various activities and amenities to entertain young guests. The club offers supervised programs and age-appropriate facilities, ensuring that children have a fun and enjoyable stay.

Chapter 8:
Common Night Destinations & Festivals in Greece

Greece is the perfect place for individuals who want to have fun while leaving their problems behind because Greeks love to party and are renowned for their distinctive and varied nightlife. Here, the nights are significantly longer and filled with wonderful experiences. There are countless ways to spend an evening, including dancing on tables at bouzouki while listening to live Greek music intermingled with DJ sets, trendy bars, outdoor parties, and DJ sets. You will undoubtedly have a good night and an outstanding experience wherever you finish up.

Nightlife in Athens

See the Acropolis illuminated up, signaling that it's time to have fun, and experience the best of Athens' nightlife! Enjoy your wonderful beverage while the music sets the mood and the city unfolds before you, luring you into the celebration.

- **Tavern Beach Bar**:You only need to know the address of Tavern Beach Bar in Possidonos to enjoy the best nightlife in Athens. This beach bar is the ideal location to appreciate the Athenian Riviera because it is situated along the water. It is the ideal party atmosphere, guaranteed to have you moving like never before, with the Chef's exclusive treats, calming drinks, upbeat music, and elegant ambiance.
- **CV Distiller**: This establishment is renowned for its extensive whiskey collection. One of Athens' most well-liked bars is this one. Therefore, if you appreciate whiskey and also crave relaxing music and prefer quiet nights, make sure to enter this opulent restaurant/bar to experience the tranquil side of Greece's typically vibrant nightlife.

Nightlife in Rhodes

Rhodes is a multicultural island that retains its distinctively Greek identity while still being a party island. Along with that, Rhodes Town itself is home to some of the top nightclubs and discos. All year long, partygoers on alcohol cruises may be seen in the vibrant clubs and bars of the well-known resort of Faliraki.

- **Paradiso Beach Club**: The Paradiso Club, one of Rhodes' most well-known nightclubs, is a place where partygoers can actually find paradise. With its attractive surroundings and lively atmosphere, this party hotspot in Rhodes will undoubtedly give you a true flavor of Greek nightlife.
- **Oasis Pool Bar**: The most distinctive location in Rhodes, with organic cuisine, a pool, lively music, and a stunning lounge space with a pool bar, displays a distinctive side of Greek nightlife that differs greatly from the city's restaurant-cum-bar and beach bar cultures.

Nightlife in Mykonos

You will find countless popular bars and clubs that are elegantly designed with a Cycladic theme and are frequented by celebrities and well-to-do Europeans. All of this will combine to create a magical evening that exudes glamor and elegance. You will go to a beachside club with a view of the Aegean as darkness falls and party there till daybreak. The music choices made by the DJ at the beach bars will have you bopping along while holding a champagne glass.

- Cavo Paradiso: The most storied club outside of town is this one. It boasts a sizable outdoor dance area that is packed with people until the early hours of the morning, when activity in Mykonos Town gradually slows down as daybreak approaches.
- Babylon: Gay and straight clubgoers frequent this well-known gay club, which is noted for its entertaining themed nights, solid mix of oldies and current top 40 songs, and regular gang shows. After a round of frantic dancing, take a drink of your cocktail.

Nightlife in Santorini

Santorini is a tranquil, lovely place by nature, but it also knows how to party hard. Simply relax with a drink in one of the many bars or dress up for one of the ultra-chic club nights organized by some of the biggest names in the DJ industry. There are many places to unwind, including diverse clubs and beach bars that play Jazz, Latin, and Soul music all night long.

- **Theros Wave Bar**: This unique, trendy pub is situated on the Vlychada Beach, which is well-known for its natural surroundings. This is regarded as the greatest location to experience a quiet and serene Greek evening while surrounded by the ocean, unique cocktails, delectable Mediterranean cuisine, and any kind of music that enhances the serene atmosphere.

- **Crystal Bar Santorini**: The Crystal Cocktail Bar, one of the most thrilling party spots in all of Greece, is a well-kept Santorini secret. This opulent location is renowned for its excellent cuisine, vivacious crowd, thrilling music, and exquisite views of the city's pearl white houses, making it one of the greatest spots to savor the spirit of Greek nightlife.

Nightlife at Thessaloniki

Young people's vitality permeates Thessaloniki's environment day and night. You will come across undiscovered gems, old cafes, quaint taverns, clubs with great music, and stunning music venues in warehouses holding live rock shows. You can place your best wager at one of the most luxurious casinos in Europe or take in some of the best Bouzouki entertainment in Greece.

- Nykis Avenue: It is actually situated where Nykis Avenue starts and Aristelous Square finishes. One of Thessaloniki's most well-known nightlife hot spots, Nykis Avenue is home to chic bars that flow out onto the waterfront and provide a one-of-a-kind vista of the Thermaikos Gulf.
- Kastra: it is the place to go if you want a special night out with someone special. This location will transport you to a bygone era where you may relax with your loved ones over a delicious glass of wine while taking in the tranquility of the most scenic and historic area of the city.

Festivals

Greece is a nation noted for its rich and varied cultural past, and celebrations have a big impact on Greek culture. These celebrations give both locals and visitors the chance to honor traditions, customs, music, dancing, and cuisine. Let's talk about some of the celebrated holidays in Greece:

1. Athens Epidaurus Festival: Held annually from May to October, the Athens Epidaurus Festival is one of the most significant cultural events in Greece. It features a wide range of performances, including theater, music, and dance, taking place in various venues, including ancient theaters like the Epidaurus Theater.

2. Easter: Easter is an essential religious festival in Greece. The celebrations start with Holy Week, marked by processions, church services, and the symbolic reenactment of the Passion of Christ. The midnight Easter Mass on Holy Saturday is a particularly significant event, with people lighting candles and fireworks to welcome the resurrection of Jesus Christ.

3. Thessaloniki International Film Festival: As one of the oldest and most prestigious film festivals in Southeast Europe, the Thessaloniki International Film Festival showcases a diverse selection of Greek and international films. It takes place annually in Thessaloniki and attracts filmmakers, industry professionals, and cinema enthusiasts from around the world.

4. Rockwave Festival: Rockwave is a popular music festival in Greece, primarily focusing on rock, alternative, and metal genres. It features both Greek and international artists and bands and takes place during the summer months in Athens. The festival offers multiple stages, creating a lively and energetic atmosphere for music lovers.

5. Kalamata Dance Festival: Held in the city of Kalamata, the Kalamata Dance Festival is dedicated to contemporary dance. It brings together renowned Greek and international dance companies, choreographers, and performers. The festival showcases a diverse range of dance styles and techniques, offering a platform for creativity and artistic expression.

6. Ohi Day (Ochi Day): Celebrated on October 28th, Ohi Day commemorates Greece's refusal to surrender to Italian forces during World War II. It is a national holiday, and festivities include parades, military processions, and cultural events across the country. Ohi Day is an occasion to honor Greek history and independence.

7. Sani Festival: Taking place in the Sani Resort in Halkidiki, the Sani Festival combines various forms of art, including music, theater, dance, and visual arts. The festival attracts renowned national and international artists, offering a diverse program of performances in a stunning natural setting.

8. Athens Technopolis Jazz Festival: This annual jazz festival in Athens celebrates the genre with performances by Greek and international jazz musicians. The festival takes place in the Technopolis cultural complex, attracting jazz enthusiasts from across Greece and beyond.

Chapter 9:
Souvenirs And Shopping In Greece

There are several alternatives accessible in Greece for travellers looking to shop. Greece is renowned for its thriving marketplaces, distinctive gifts, and regional goods. Here are some locations in Greece where tourists like to shop:

1. Plaka, Athens: Plaka is a historic neighborhood in Athens known for its narrow streets, traditional houses, and numerous shops. Here, you'll find a wide range of items such as jewelry, ceramics, leather goods, traditional Greek clothing, and souvenirs.
2. Monastiraki Flea Market, Athens: Located near the ancient ruins of Athens, Monastiraki is a bustling flea market where you can find all sorts of treasures. From antique furniture and vintage clothing to handmade crafts and artwork, this market offers a unique shopping experience.
3. Ermou Street, Athens: Ermou Street is one of the main shopping streets in Athens, offering a mix of high-end boutiques, international brands, and local shops. It's a great place to explore if you're looking for fashion, accessories, and cosmetics.
4. Mykonos Town: Mykonos is known for its luxury boutiques, designer shops, and trendy fashion. The narrow streets of Mykonos Town are lined with fashion-forward clothing, jewelry, and unique gifts. It's a popular destination for fashion-conscious tourists.
5. Santorini: The picturesque island of Santorini is famous for its stunning views and charming villages. Oia and Fira are the main shopping hubs where you'll find boutiques selling handmade jewelry, local artwork, traditional textiles, and Santorini's famous wine.
6. Rhodes Old Town: The medieval town of Rhodes offers an enchanting shopping experience. Its cobbled streets are home to shops selling handmade ceramics, rugs, spices, olive oil, and local products. The Street of the Knights is particularly known for its boutiques.

7. Chania Old Town, Crete: Chania's Old Town is a maze of narrow streets filled with shops selling traditional Cretan products. You can find locally produced olive oil, herbs, wines, honey, and handmade crafts like ceramics and textiles.
8. Thessaloniki: Greece's second-largest city, Thessaloniki, is a vibrant shopping destination. Tsimiski Street and Mitropoleos Street are popular shopping streets, offering a mix of high-end stores, international brands, and local shops selling clothing, accessories, and more.

The mementos you purchase will show off Greek history and culture. Shopaholics will find paradise in neighborhoods like Monastiraki and Plaka, where they can purchase anything from leather sandals to Komboloi to several types of olive oils and much more. The following are the must-purchase trinkets while visiting Greece:

Fresh Herbs

Greece's population chooses more conventional and natural pharmaceutical solutions because they have faith in their health care system. You can treat your condition with a variety of herbs, each with unique properties. Chamomile is one such herb that can help you with any problem, whereas lavender can be used to help you relax and the Cretan lemon balm is wonderful for treating depression. These herbs are widespread across Greece. These can potentially rank among the best souvenirs from your vacation to Greece to give as gifts. Oregano, saffron, thyme, and many other herbs are also simple to locate. Look for the well-known feta cheese herb; it is incredibly delicious and pairs nicely with cheese and bread.

Olive Oil Products

Greece is well-known for its olives and olive oil around the globe. Due to its association with the goddess Athena, olives represent peace and wealth in Greece. Simply put, Greek olives are the greatest. Different types of olives can be purchased vacuum-packed, making them ideal for giving to your colleagues. Olive oil comes in a variety of qualities and quantities and is incredibly tasty. Nearly all Greek foods and recipes call for virgin olive oil. In addition, olive oil is used to make a variety of items, including cosmetics, medicines, and even soaps. Additionally, you may purchase olives from farms and stores, and cookware made of olive tree wood makes a great keepsake.

Handmade Backgammon Set

Backgammon is one of the most played board games in Greece, and you can often see older people and students playing it while sipping coffee at more formal coffee shops. It's a fun game that also looks great in homes. Porters, Plakoyto, and Fevga can be played on this board, also known as the Tavli. Tavli is a fantastic way to spend time with your friends because the rules are simple and simple to learn, and it also ensures that you will have quality time with your partner. Purchase it as a family gift so that you may all enjoy it.

Blue Eye

Greek folklore holds that wearing blue eyes will shield you from the evil eye. The well-known talisman known as the blue eye is said to repel any unfavorable glances and return them back to the person casting them. It has been cited in Hesiod's writings and is incredibly common in Greek folklore. It comes in a variety of shapes, primarily jewelry but also other objects.

Greek Wine

Greece vacations aren't complete without trying the local wines. The highest caliber wines are available here. White wines should be the finest on the cooler islands since they have a crisp flavor, a dry flavor, and a high acidity. This is a result of the vineyards being nearly always exposed to strong winds and chilly nighttime temperatures. And head to the northwest region if you're seeking for red wines. Bring some of the top Greek wines to make your peers happy.

Mastiha

This is a natural resin obtained from the mastic trees of Chios Island. Mastiha, the earliest chewing gum ever created, has been utilized for its therapeutic and pharmacological benefits ever since Greek antiquity. Products of Mastiha are very famous in Greece. You will find different products with the taste of Mastiha such as liquor, traditional products and cosmetics. It is a special and enjoyable memento for you, your friends, and family.

Bouzouki

If you enjoy music, you will undoubtedly adore the exquisite Bouzouki instrument. Greeks hold a very special place in their hearts for this musical instrument. One of the most well-known musical instruments in Greece is the bouzouki, a long-necked plucked instrument. Therefore, you may undoubtedly obtain one from Greece, and the sound of this item is exquisite. Additionally, you can purchase the miniature versions if you'd prefer a more affordable and compact option.

Leather Sandals

one of the most famous and desirable items to purchase in Greece. These sandals are a must-have memento from Greece because they go with virtually anything. To replicate the sandals used by the ancient Greeks, their design is relatively straightforward. The most popular footwear among tourists is probably leather sandals, which are popular among locals and have a slight classical Greek influence. They can be found in a variety of designs and colors to suit your taste and preferences. They are available in various unique colors and styles at stores all over the world.

Conclusion

Greece is a small nation in Southeastern Europe where one of the world's greatest civilizations flourished more than 2000 years ago. It is a popular tourist destination due to its geographically appealing location and ancient culture, which has had a significant influence on the arts, language, philosophy, politics and the Olympics. It is known for its religious and architectural diversity. Greece is one of Europe's prime destinations due to its countless islands, sandy beaches, ancient archaeological sites and Mediterranean climate. It is home to the world's third largest producer of olive oil and Mediterranean cuisine. Visitors can enjoy Delphi, Santorini and Mykonos, as well as Delphi's 18 UNESCO World Heritage Sites and Santorini's spectacular sunsets. However, it is only by being present physically in the country that one can truly understand the place.

Printed by BoD˜in Norderstedt, Germany